M000191855

# Brewing Storms

# Brewing Storms

A.M. RAMZY

DAYBREAK PRESS

2014

Brewing Storms
All Rights Reserved © 2014 by A.M. Ramzy

Published by:
Daybreak Press
St. Paul, Minnesota, USA

ISBN: 978-0-9906259-2-6
Library of Congress Control Number: 2014948324


Cover Image: Paths Crossing by Sean R. Heavy
Cover, design and typesetting by scholarlytype.com


Printed in the United States of America

**For my Mother**

who was an anchor during my storms, and
whose shelter I miss deeply.

# Contents

# Acknowledgments

I am indebted to many people who contributed to making this collection of poems a possibility, including:

My mother, who did not live to see this book published but whose company always provided me with warmth and safe harbour in all weathers, I pray she now rests in eternal sunshine;

my father, whose phenomenal ambition and drive are a continuous source of motivation for me, and who has supported me in my interests and encouraged me from a young age to write, and for whom this book is about ten years late in coming;

Anse Tamara, my spiritual guide, mentor, lighthouse, who both inspired and nurtured my journey and the poems that speak of it from the very first piece I showed her as we sat in Damascus what seems a lifetime ago;

my sister, Hannah, whose moral and emotional support is a huge blessing, who has seen me through many a murky moment and whose strength and boundless consideration for others I admire more than I can express;

my brothers, Ibrahim and Abdullah, who keep me on my toes, and Hossain, whose investment in my dreams I hope to one day repay;

my dear grandparents, whose love, warmth and welcome mean so much to me, and who hold a treasured place in my life and heart, and my aunts, uncles and all my cousins whose care and company I cherish and whom I'm blessed to call my family;

Najiyah Maxfield-Helwani, who selflessly set apart hours of her time to edit and critique my writing and put up with endless pestering on my part, all of which she did with an enthusiasm and energy that made the task a joy;

Nusaiba Imady, whose opinion, expertise and friendship I highly prize but of whose praise I never feel quite worthy;

Eamaan Rabbat, who 'gets it', and to whom I'd send these poems as a means of communication, and whose presence on my path has been a Godsend, and my travelling companions, Nishat, Sunia and Saimah and all the other Geese and Rabata sisters, who feature in amongst these lines (perhaps unbeknownst to them), and without whom there would have been far fewer sunny patches along the way.

It, of course, goes without saying that I am deeply grateful to my Creator for every page and every word that has finally come together, and for leading me to a path upon which even in the dark times there is light.

# Foreword

**M**OST OFTEN SEEN IN the relationship between Rumi and Shams, the give and take between teacher and student is more than just a passing on of knowledge. It is a fighting of the *nafs*, a stretching of emotion, and sometimes a painful confusion as the student struggles to learn and memorize sacred texts, to change her bad habits and hone her character, and to make broad steps forward on the path of Islam.

The stories of men, as seeker and teacher, are found in the pages of heritage texts and literary works, but the stories of women are rare. *Brewing Storms* provides a window into a short span of one young woman's spiritual road. The use of poetry allows every reader to experience the journey in her own way, use some of the words and phrases to explain her own emotions, and explore new avenues of understanding and compassion.

*Brewing Storms* is a collection of poetry written by a natural poet, who has been influenced by the Arabic and Persian poetry and language she soaked up at Oxford University and during her short, intense time in Damascus, Syria.

I hope that as you read her work, you will catch a glimpse of this path for yourself, and perhaps your brewing storms will find their sun, clouds, rain, storms, and sun again.

Anse Tamara Gray

# Author's Introduction

THE WEATHER SYSTEMS OF the soul come in many shades. There are the vibrant rays of joy that cut through the clouds, the thunder of deep fears, the lightening strikes of guilt and remorse, the rains of relief. Most prominent in this collection are the storms, the tempests of change.

A storm is defined as 'a disturbance of the normal condition of the atmosphere, manifesting itself by winds of unusual force or direction.'[1] For the first two decades of my life I had done my best to avoid storms, to steer clear of any disturbances in my internal atmosphere. I saw storms as a sign of destruction, of havoc. I learned in early 2010 whilst living in Damascus, however, that this was not true. Storms are a sign of change. And hesitantly I embraced them. Those unusual winds pushed me in a direction I never knew existed, cleared out the dry leaves of seasons past that stifled new shoots. They eroded facades and battered down walls. They cleared the air of tension, of doubt, of anxiety. I learned to welcome each storm as it brewed. I learned to sense the growing restlessness of the breeze, greet the congregation of clouds overhead, and read the words the lightning etched across my darkness.

I wrote the poems in this collection as an attempt to convey some of the atmospheric changes I experienced as I embarked on a journey of spiritual growth. There were some pieces I hesitated to include, afraid that my darkness might reflect badly on the route I had set myself upon. I opted for honesty, with the realisation that any darkness was my own, that it had been there, that dawn had broken and would continue to do so, and that, as a human being, my past and present are a canvas of dark and light, and that the point of the path was to illuminate the

---

1   "storms", Random House Dictionary, New York: Random House, Inc. 2014. Dictionary.com accessed on 13 July 2014.

shadows. So you'll find them in here, along with the expressions of deep, profound, unfathomable joy, of a type known only to the rain-drenched traveller when the rays of warmth finally arrive and reach right through to her bones.

Storms are often strenuous. Gripped by the ferocious winds of thoughts and fears, soaked through with heavy drops of realisation, you long for an end, for sunlight, for warmth, for clarity. After weathering the storm, you appreciate the sun all the more when it comes. For it always comes.

Change is brewed. It does not happen suddenly. Slowly, as the temperature increases and your soul is left to steep, the goodness, the flavour, the intensity is released. The word 'storm' itself comes from the root 'to swirl', and just as the grains of coffee, the leaves of tea whirl in the pot, just as the dervish twirls, just as the storm clouds circle over head, so does change churn inside until it settles into your being. It is not always an easy process. Jalal al-Din Rumi, who some might call the foremost poet of the path, attested to this again and again: "If you are irritated by every rub, how will your mirror be polished?" If we run from every storm, how will our horizon ever become clear?

A.M. Ramzy
Oxford, UK
July 2014

xvi

# Brewing Storms

# Into the Unknown

My future is a fitful hallucination
Fed by the ecstasies of the present
Only to disappear when sobering reality returns to haunt me.
I rummage frantically in the lost property box of dreams
To find one that fits
So I may join the ranks...
I find none.
I swim the lagoon of uncertainty alone.

# Sickness

In the sickness that embraced me
I coughed up my heart
And watched as my veins went trailing
Off into the dark.
A shadow of a shell,
I stood beside the road
And in my private hell
Out my spirits flowed.
I didn't see them leave
Though I felt a sudden chill
As I realised I was empty
And so fatally ill.
No matter how many clothes
I shrouded round my skin
Nor how many lights I lit
The darkness was within.

# Speak to Me

Speak to me the songs of my silent soul.
Enliven the scattered sands of far-off lands
In which I plant my fingers.
Whisper to me the long vowels of the breeze
And the diphthongs of the swallows.
Teach me to strum on my vocal chords
With my newly rooted hands,
And beat the taut skin over my aching heart
In harmony with who I am.

# Leap of Faith

O heart, so tangled and torn
And wanting,
In denial, creeping forth
Then shying so far away.
Don't be afraid, little heart
I know you're beating fast;
It's all so new
Out here
Over there
Across the fence...
Yes, the grass is greener here
It grows taller here
Problems are so much smaller here
Because there are bigger things
Beautiful things.
Faith gives you wings!
You say you have none
But make the jump,
I'll catch you! Come!
Across the fence
Out here
Over there.
I promise you, little heart
God will give you a pair,
And you'll realise
You knew all along
How to fly.

# Torn

How is it possible to be so attached to you
And yet be running in the other direction?

How is it possible to feel so full of emotions
And yet so empty?

My body wears armour
Yet my insides bleed.

My heart is wet with tears
But my eyes are stone dry.

I'm dying to talk to you
But I have nothing to say.

Break the silence
To mend me.

Tie the bonds
To set me free.

# Clouded Vision

Gazing at the sky one day
A handsome cloud drifted my way.
Its misty beauty captured me
Enraptured me, and in a flurry
Of blind desire I was mesmerised
In a yearning gaze I was crystallised…
In the breezeless serenity of that day
I sat, and my mind sang the time away
And while the birds chirped in time to my heart's every beat
Night came to trade my ambrosia for sleep.
To dispel my fear the cloud whispered sweetly
That when morning came, it would still be there to greet me.
But when I awoke, as the light slowly leaked
From horizon's great font, I was met with deceit.
For the cloud had rode off, gliding free, flying wild
To traverse deep blue skies and seduce the next child.
I searched for a trace of that cloud every day
In each hollow form that floated my way.
I fell fleetingly in love with so many a wisp
Praying to rediscover that unmistakable bliss.
But each day my feeble hopes would be left in tatters, undone
My silhouette dark, crumbled ruins I'd become
For not once had I noticed, in my quest for that 'one'
That each flimsy cloud had been blocking the Sun.

# A Fortress of Phrases

I built a fortress of phrases
On a mountain of pages
And a wreath of words
Fell low upon my brow.
I sung hymns to eloquence
Composed odes to fluency
Filled the air with rhythms and rhymes
Till my tongue became parched
And I realised
As I opened my eyes
That the thirst of the soul
Is quenched by the heart.

# A Losing Battle

The stupid soldier fights on.
He is a coward,
The one with his sword drawn.
Easily identifiable,
He perspires zeal -
His passion misplaced.
An aspiring general
With no vision.
A gutless cur,
His eyes glazed red.
He is blinded
By the glint of his own sword.
He rages forth,
Impatient to prove his bravery
If only to himself.
He understands not,
This soldier,
That the move that takes the most courage
Is to surrender.

# Baggage Reclaim

A elliptical strip of grey, endlessly rotating...
The nowhere going track
Of baggage accumulating,
An endless race, behind a sidetracked face...
I follow the signs aimlessly
To collect what weighs me down
And then I stand there waiting
For my turn to come around.
Wouldn't life be easier if all we had to do
Was head off the plane and out the door
Nothing to drag across the floors?
Who's to say because it once was yours
That you can't stop those bags, your departure prolonging,
And rid yourself of those 'personal belongings'?
So, when they've checked your face against your name,
Why not free yourself and walk on by
The signs to 'Baggage Reclaim'?

# Poetry and I

What am I
But a poem as yet unwritten, unread
A song as yet unsung
Whose lines tremble inside me
Whose beat is released in the uncontrollable rhythm
    of sobs and sighs.
I find life only on your lips
From which I am freed
Leaving me
Formed in thin air.
What am I
But a breath as yet unbreathed
Stifled by the thickness
Of the echoes of I don't know
I don't know
Strangled by streams of unexplainable tears.
The pen is my poet
The ink is my blood
My parchment is air
My words are notes
And I am the poetry
As yet unformed, unwritten, unsaid, unsung.

# Elevated

Tentatively, I step inside
Your elevator.

The invitation hung,
I must admit,
Before I was brave enough
To take the leap.

I'm new to this building.

I catch the lift on my floor
Where it arrives
Descended from greater heights,
An upper level.

It's glass,
Your elevator.
You push the buttons,
Switch us on.
The world beneath
Fades away
As we climb...

We reach our destination.
Doors open.
I'm bathed in light -
Elevated.

I don't know how long I stay
But somewhere in the distance

Time chimes
Catching up with me

And I must return
To my level.

But the invitation
Still stands.

I may return
To your welcome
On the upper floor
Of this skyscraper.

Only this time
I must take the stairs.

# Being

Dancing in the palm of your hand,
Cradled in your arms, I hear you breathe
Clutching your fingertips, I trace the swirls
That left their prints on me.

Skipping along in your shadow
Embraced by the warmth that it casts,
Resting my cheek on your shoulder
Firmly fixed in your grasp.

Caught in your glance and held in a trance
Of weightlessness, crystal clear seeing
Crying tears of joy and deep cleansing
Holding your hand and fleetingly
Being.

# A Rush of Colour to the Heart

A rush of colour to the heart
Vivid, clear, beautiful
Overwhelming, overpowering
Showering my spirit
With droplets of the sky in all its shades
The Artist's paintbrush stirring
Swirling, whirling
Transforming blacks and whites
Into rainbows
That beat around my body
A kaleidoscope cascade

# Alive

Take my hand and hold it tight, tighter still, don't let go...

Let me sit close by your side and let your energy flow
Into my bones, my blood, my self, my being and my soul,
Stick me back with gentleness so once again I'm whole.

Let me breathe the air around you,
Bathe in your light so I can see,
And remember where I'm going, and who I want to be.

Take me in your arms, encompass me with care,
Lend me conviction and encouragement
Not just for me, to share.

Let me raise my head to meet your gaze,
And from your eyes keep pouring
The strength and love and tenderness
So I might feel my heart restoring.

I want to go to greater depths,
Give me the strength to dive.

I want to go to greater heights,
Give me the wings to fly.

I want to reach new levels, new peaks,
Give me the strength to strive.

Let me rest my head upon your chest
To fill up, reenergize.

And let me hear your heartbeat,
To remind me I'm alive...

# Solitude

The quiet fullness of the air,
The invigorating surge of silence,
The relief of being alone,
The tranquility of not.

# Lullaby Temptress

Sleep, you temptress
Dancing before me in your dark, velvety gown
Caressing my eyelids
With heavy strokes
Numbing my thoughts into dreams...

I will not succumb
To your beckoning
The invitation to your quilted realm.

I shall not be seduced
By your cradling embrace
Your sweetly whispered lullabies
Carrying me to the world
Behind my shuttered eyes...

Be gone, thief!
I shall not let you steal my solace
It is not yours to take.
For this time is precious
This night is mine.

# Rapture

I could burst into a million tiny pieces
And sprinkle all that burns inside me
Amongst the stars

I could sit with you for hours on end
And say so much
Without saying a word

I could lose myself in your gaze
And dance in the joy
Of being guided

I could scatter myself across the earth
So birds may feed from me
And sing the songs of my heart that you silently taught me

I could lie on the shore of eternity
And let wave after wave after wave
Wash me into the expanse of breathing

I could die, holding your hand, in that moment
Of pure pulsating bliss, that inkling of what it is
To be alive

# Fresh Bubblegum

I want to
Lie in a field
And chew fresh bubblegum
Let the sunlight pouring down
Soak into my skin.

I want to
Revel in the flavour of freedom
Sniff the pure scent of serenity
Be cradled in the arms of solitude.

I want to
Close my eyes and watch the shapes beneath my lids
And sway to the intoxicating melodies of birdsong
Applaud the crickets for their midnight serenade.

I want to
See shapes in the clouds
Pull faces at the moon
And breathe in the bliss they exhale.

I want to
Lose count of the stars strewn across a dense blue sky
Bathe in the raindrops
And be absorbed by the quenched earth.

I want to
Lie in a field
And chew fresh bubblegum.

# Incoherence

The incoherence of love:
A lucid, clear and free flowing stream
Of vivid silence
Only those
Only those
Who have felt it can hear it babble as it gushes
    through the brook.
In the asylum of rational thought
They play with spaghetti letters
And tell me this is how to speak
One day
One day
You'll wash away that mess in that stream
Or eat your words.
Either way, by then
I hope to be far away
Carried out towards the sea.

# Marvelous Medicines

There are keys
To a world unseen
To the inner dimensions of your inner being
A tongue-span
Heart-span
A heartbeat away
That make your tales of magic seem child's play
Your pills and brews and potions and spells
Make the heart shrivel, and the mind swell.
But these
Remedies
That dance in the breeze
That rest
Upon crests
Of wave after wave
It's these you crave
For your darkness, your ailments,
When you feel torn or upset
They're free for the taking
They'll stop that heart aching
He has supplied them
You just haven't tried them
Applied them
Yet.

# Breaking Rocks

I face the boulder
In my path
Foreboding, vast, dark.

I could walk around this boulder, I know
But that would lead me
On a lesser path.

So I stand
Pick axe in hand
And strike.

Sparks fly.

Tick, tick, tick
Away I chip
My muscles ache
From the countless hits.

I hack, attack
Wield every weapon I've got
At this rock.

Every chip, drip
Wears away at this
Mountain
I'm trying to climb.

Until one day I stand
Pick axe in hand
Seeing no boulder
Just a pile of sand

That I brush away
Into the hourglass of my life
And watch it slip
Into the past.

And I step forward
Stronger.

# Memories of a Mountain

That girl
Trembling ever so slightly
Stood on the side of a mountain
Her blindfold removed
Catching her breath in the breeze
Eyes sparkling wide
Drinking in the glittering expanse
Before, beneath, above her
That girl whose mouth was awash
With bread and cheesecake
Digested with laughter
And an ecstasy and awe, oh so sweet
Whose hands and heart
Were so full of love
She felt she could scoop up stars
To wash down a fulfilling night
Felt she could run her fingers
Along the soft fabric of peace
And draw it close around her
Sleep on a woven mat
Of unwhispered words, velvet thoughts,
And the tight squeeze of a certain hand
That girl felt she could live that night
On the mountain forever
That girl...

# Why can't the water always taste like this?

Even the water tastes sweeter here
My thoughts are kinder to me
And my demons have disappeared.
I am confused by the clarity.
I wonder who I was
And who I thought you were...
For now that you're here,
And everything is clear
The past is a haze
And yet the present seems a dream
And I wonder,
If this is who I am, then who have I been?
And I worry
That this is just a fleeting sip of bliss
And that when you're gone
I'll stray back into the abyss...
Why can't the water always taste like this?

# On Departure

It will hurt again, I know
The tears will fall again so
Fluidly, you having melted the ice
That was my soul, and tomorrow's
Tomorrow will come again
Again, I know.

I wish I could write you
Into the paperback book of my life
In tear proof ink so
That when the time comes
For this chapter to close
I can put the pages to my nose
And breathe in your words
And stroke the softness of the paper
Wherein there still lingers
The touch of your cashmere fingers
Remember the beginning
And the crisp clean start
Relive the openings and know
That the plot always progresses
That's how all stories go.

It will hurt again, I know
But the full stops I scratched
You've smoothed to commas
So the sentences still flow
And you will be there till the final line
Writing my story with me, helping it grow

And I'll sign your name upon the hardback cover
So that everyone will know.

# The Moon

Reclining on illuminated clouds
Rests the moon.
A shifting smile, sharing its borrowed light
With those skiving sleep.
A piercing slice through the deep inky blackness
Reflecting a ray from worlds away.
Its creamy brightness a softened beam
From a blazing source
On the other side of the world.
Its slimmed curves an indicator
Of an ancient past and an ever disappearing present.
Its incomplete form,
The pitch black shadow of the earth on its clean white surface,
A reminder of how this world can plunge us into darkness.
But a reminder as well
To share what little light we have.

# Remembrance

Rasping breaths
And syllables stressed
By tongues and lungs,
Arteries strummed to new beats.
The Word reverberates
As fingers shake,
Wooden beads of sweat
And tears that should have already fallen.
Calling out a Name
Searching for a strand
And a wide-palmed hand
Across the ocean in a familiar land.
Awaiting an answer, a lift, a paradigm shift
A sign in response to my stolen gift...
Like doves of breath
Released from throat to air
Each with a letter repeated yet rare
Knowing they'll be heard
Because I know
You're there.

# I found a pebble

I found a pebble on the beach
The shape and size of perfection
It sparkled and twinkled in the sun
And put to shame my past collection.
But when I bent to pick it up
To take it away and make it mine
There came a wave which pulled it away
And I, no more, that pebble could find.
I passed days and nights sat on the shore,
Waves of salt water before me, within
Until one day I understood
And, with a leap, I jumped right in.
Surrounded by that great expanse,
That clear, filled, cleansing space
Being in that sea, I knew,
We were, at last, in the same place.

# Missing

The ripping, tearing, wrenching
After having waited so long
A hole filled with longing
A solid pain leaks into the bliss.

The struggle through each day
The soaring, crawling
Knowing that the ebbs and flows of time
Will reunite our hands and hearts
Only for them to be pulled apart
As oceans separate us once more.

Whilst you stand here beside me
And your voice resounds inside me
Still I long, I yearn, I plead
For your embrace, a glimpse of your face
The soothing sound of your heartbeat
And our fingers interlaced...
I miss you.

# Back to the Grind

Grinding away
At thoughts, at words
Till blisters form on my brain
My eyes stare sore
My finger bones brittle
To produce perfect pieces on smooth clean paper
Whilst my insides have crumpled
A mass of scribbles.

# Music

Sweet liquid melodies
Run riddles through my veins
Poured into my soul
They twist aches into pains.
Stirring, they reach my heart
Once again, once more
Where they play and adventure
Tear open, explore
Revisit closed doors,
Leave taps running free
Turn a basin of emotions
Into a swarming sea.
Any resistance dissolved
They melt all supports
Leaving me crumbling
In a pool of my thoughts.

# Yearning

There's so much more I want to say,
But yet again my tongue is silent.

My heart screams out 'cooperate!'
My emotions, feelings violent.

The thunder, lightning, storms inside
Invisible on the surface.

The only window to my soul,
My eyes, I lower on purpose.

The tears and sobs well up inside
In danger of overflowing.

I open my mouth to try to speak,
But you're already going...

To say 'come back' is selfish
Though I scream it out inside.

I still haven't learned my lesson:
Connect your heart, your tongue, don't hide.

# Living Turmoil

That heavy feeling you get
When your heart is anchored
Yet all you want to do is sail on
With the wind at your back
Full steam ahead.

That burning feeling you get
When your cheeks are on fire
From the heat of the embarrassment
You caused by stoking the flames
Of that roaring furnace of transgression.

That sinking feeling you get
When the guts of your heart plummet
Resting on its floor
In a hot sorry heap
Of failure.

That tortured feeling you get
When your inner self goes reeling
From the stabs to your conscience,
From the wounds you have caused.

That dying feeling you get
When you shrivel inside
And you just want to be buried
In the hole that you've dug yourself.

Mean only one thing:
You're alive.

# Full

Give me a cup half full of peace of mind
A hand sandwich
Yours, mine, yours, mine, yours, mine
A side helping, or hindering, of indigestible emotions
And a napkin for the blood, sweat and tears.

Perhaps Alexander did find the Elixir of Life
But knowing there was someone waiting on the other side
  of knowledge
He let it slip, before his men, midst those treacherous lands
Drop by drop onto the sand
Where once a year
Every year
In the dead of night there grows a rose
That dies at sunrise.

I threw a branch off a bridge
Watched the ripples waving at me in endless rings
And laughed as I waited at the other side
For it to come into view.
I missed it.
The river swelled with my tears
And the banks of memories became saturated
Leaving a tide mark every time -
New target, past limit, constant reminder.

Perhaps the Elixir that seeped through Alexander's grasp
Was nothing but water
Which fell on a gasping
Seed.

Buried.
And all it needed was a drop
To fill it with life.

# Strings Attached

Trying to plait together
The ropes that are pulling me apart
So they may become a steadfast chord
To lead me along my path
And stop twisting into the tightening noose
That's strangling my heart.

# Missing Melodies

Scrabbling for the strings
Desperately groping in the dark
Losing my place, starting again
Reaching up and out
Into the silence
Of the dying hours of night.

The heavy emptiness stares back
A frustration growing
The light evading me
Click, click, tick
Seconds and beads fall away
I battle myself
Stumble between heart, mind and sleep
Batting away thoughts as my eyelids close
Or are they open?
It's so dark.

I hear the birds singing their praises
Mine are so out of tune
Where is the melody that sang with my heartbeats?
Where are the sighs the brought the chorus to life?
I claw at the drums, straining the chords,
Wincing at the shrill attempts,
Mind aching, heart vacant
But still playing
Feebly playing.

# Because I don't know the answer...

Sometimes
There is just so much on your mind
That you start sinking
Under all the thinking
Life's icebergs
Have halted your plain sailing
You're flailing
Each and every synapse flicker
Makes your heart beat quicker
But you're failing
To keep a straight head
When the road seems so skewed
And the never-ending feud
Between you, yourself and you
Perpetuates
An unfriendly stalemate
Since you're all unique
But one of a kind
And you hate
That this tangled mass of
Lines of thought
Never seems to unwind
So please
Don't ask me
"What's on your mind?"

# I know…

I know you're there
But I don't feel like I'm with you

I know you can feel my heartbeat
But I don't feel your finger on my pulse

I know you can hear me silently speaking
But I can't feel you listening

I know you're carrying me
But I still feel so heavy

I know you're holding my hand
But I feel like I'm clutching at air

I know you shouldn't have to
But please just say 'I'm here...'

# On Finding No Words

As sheer irritation coils round my heart
Strangling it more than the words that it chokes on,

As desperation claws frantically at the towering walls
Of a closely guarded fortress of feelings,

As anger flicks across tear stained eyes
At fingers failing to sing in tune
With the bursting odes of an anguished soul...

I put my pen down
On a blank page.

# Half-caste

Suddenly there's a hole
And I'm half
The blood of two empires runs in my veins
Straddles civilisations
Yet I taste only the memories and longing of adopted children
I hear the babbling brooks only through storybooks
And I smell the musty streets, the spices, sweets
From aromatic words quivering in the throats of branded travellers
A confluence of histories shapes my present
Mixed into the mould of my potential form
Every essence of my foreign being
Strives to claim words that should be mine
Purchased by others who have set foot in my home
Away from home
To which I may one day return
Embrace, see, savour, taste
And yet still never belong.

# Blind Man's Stride

Partially sighted
And senses failing,
Crashing and stumbling,
Thrashing and fumbling,
Sometimes enraged
And other times just confused,
Upsetting those precious things around me
As I look for a door.
Clumsy and unrefined,
Valuables break to my left, to my right;
Splinters of my handiwork
Embedding themselves in me
Devastation and havoc wreaked -
I must, I must
Take time to think and stop
Living like a bull
In a china shop.

# A High Price

The fine sands of the wrong path
Are soft underfoot.
The tingle of rebellion
Ripples through every muscle.
Hungry eyes devour
Every morsel hitherto denied.
The tang of false freedom
Sends saliva rushing in
To savour
Digest the forbidden fruit
Filling up a craving soul.
Ravenous
Seeking sustenance
In the arid river beds
Filled with water of the elusive mirage.
Desire grows as it is quenched
The ever-thirsty spirit
Remains unslaked.
One foot off the path
And a chasm is cleft in the world,
The darkness seeps through
Enchanting.
An existence
Fulfilling the void
Fulfillingly void.
An unreality
Where the soul is unwittingly emancipated into slavery
Lashed to the world

Chained to the dust
Traded at any cost
In the marketplace of empty lives
And human shells.

# Hell's Cacophony

An orgy of words,
Savouring the flesh
As it is ripped from the opponent's back,
Succulent revenge
Unbeknownst to them.
Slashing, tearing, chewing, spitting
Revelling in the attack,
Ears hungry for more
Infected by the pestilence
Contagious, vulgar.
Desperate for the ecstasy
Of the one sided victory
Tasting the sweetness of the spite
On the tip of the tongue
As it cuts deeper
Shredding honour, dignity, trust
Scarring the heart
With every vicious thrust.

# The Enemy Within

The groping, clutching, snatching,
Twisting, turning, churning
Ropes of tangled feelings
On the surface hide
Knotted by the green-eyed monster
That lurks inside.
It feeds off false needs
Buried in pleasure, it lies in wait
Ready for the bait
Snarling at the sharing
The diverted attention, love, caring
The green eyes stare, glaring
Burning, yearning
For what isn't mine.
Then on a feast of phony deprivation
It sits alone to dine.
Flecks of greed and gluttony
Rimmed with an insatiability
Green eyes brim with scaly tears
Supplying a sea of envy
Where it wallows in false fears
Clawing at the walls of my heart
Tearing it down, pulling it apart
To drown in waves of flames.
For the stony green-eyed monster
Cannot bear to hear others' names.

# Another Blow

Don't plunge the dagger deeper
With your laughter and your smiles
Put away the silver platter
With which you offer up your work
Don't twist the blade with your good deeds
Don't fire the arrows with your times of need
Don't claw at me.
I'm at war with me.
I'm killing myself inside
Trying, oh so desperately, to hide
These feelings that are not mine
But which taint the bond between us all the same
It's just so hard for me
Still
To hear your name.

# Gaps

The silence scares me
Hours, days, weeks of blissful pain
The sharp sting of not knowing when I'll see you again
Have been numbed by…

And the sea is calm
The thunder and lightening of agony
The heart wrenching, entrenching, sweet waves of tragedy
Were pacified by…

The rivers, the brooks, the streams
Torrents of tears by day and in dreams
Were dried by…

The light, the flames, the hope
The fire in my palms from clinging to the rope
Were dimmed by…

I'm empty, I'm bare, I'm cold and I'm scared
And I'm going deaf, I'm going dumb, I can't see, I feel numb
I…

Shouldn't be here.
It was only ever supposed to be
You
Who filled in the gaps.

# So Long

It's been a long time
Many miles, many footsteps, many hand spans
Ago
Tears would be my pillow and pain my only comfort
Vivid pictures, now polaroids
Crisp clean sounds only crumpled reverberations read from
   notebooks
It's been such a long time
Many oceans, many lands, many time zones
Ago
I tinkered with my wind up character and it marched smoothly
   on the marble floors and dusty streets
Now nothing but a mass of cogs and uncompressed springs, and
   a shell face
Life has become a game of soldiers since then
It's been such a very long time
It has, it is, it was
Many days, many nights, many blinks, many breaths, many lives
Ago

# Ticking Boxes

Dusty words and
Wrinkled sound waves
Balding models
Shrinking fashions
Dustbins full of empty rhetoric
Revolting movements
Fitful flashing images
Day after day after night
Antiquated fun
Reduced, reused, recycled
Acrylic food
Plastic attire
A stinking quagmire
Of normality
Sleeping on a bed of springs
Six feet under
A roof of clay
Shuffling
From box to box to box
Connecting dots
Who's not?
To unravel a puzzle
That's a part of me
This room's full of the smell of old memories
From a time gone by
When life's curtains were open.
The garden runs wild
Around a house

With a clay roof
Which the ivy has reclaimed
While I sit
And flit
From box to box to box.

# Playing the Part

I talk to you of little things
Of scissors, paper, glue and string
Of making models, paper planes
I parcel up my hidden pains
And store them deep in my heart
Scared that the darkness will seep
Out and leave a mark
On the clean white reputation
I've been trying so hard to present
Truth is, it all fell through
When you went.
And that clean white sheet
Is stained and burned
And all my toiling and efforts have turned
To remembering, reliving
Not moving on, and giving
I smile and I laugh and I jest and I joke
But the truth is they're mostly lies
Aided by each and every stroke
With which my pen caresses
A crumpled page.
My world's a stage
And I play, play, play at being
In the hope that you're not seeing
How my wasted efforts are spent
Because the truth is
I became a liar
As soon as you went.

# Shattered

Staring
With deadened eyes
And an old, cold soul
And the taste of broken plates
On the tongue
Bitter.
Dying for someone
With hands outstretched, shoulders braced
Knees bent and a caring face
To ask
'How are you?'
So you can tell them you're tired
Of picking up shattered smiles
And hanging them back on cheeks
Only to fall off again
As soon as mouths are opened.
The silence tense and taught
Threatening to snap at any second.
Praying this is all a dream
And that the screams
Are only the bleeps of the alarm clock
The pulse of a bright new dawn.
Damn.
What's the price of normality?
Believe me I'll pay
Because it's so hard to pull yourself together
When you're being torn apart every
Single
Day.

# Not in Denial

The clock ticks too fast
Showers, endless showers
The grip of reality tightens on my shoulders
But I cannot turn around
Tears ripped out in anger
Spit sticky from silent screaming.
A recurring ring, repeated rhetoric.
I wrapped my heart in clingfilm
It's in a fridge somewhere
To be reheated someday
When we cross 'that bridge'.
Endless showers and recurring rings
So many clocks
Ticking too fast.

# Liars

Most of us are liars
But we don't dare admit it
We chop and dice and spread the truth
We cut and halve and split it
And we smear a small piece
Over our faces in a smile
But we forget that in truth
It only stays on a while
And in the flicker of a flash of pain
In the sudden downpour of cold rain
You don't realise your sadness has stained
Your face
Your little lies cannot hide the trace
But because you know that I'm lying too
Even though you can see through
My guise, you won't admit it
Because then we'd both have to shed our masks
And, oh dear Lord, what a terrible task
My painted face, it has to last.
I will not permit it.

# In the flesh

I shall peel off my skin
And inflate it
So you can have the version you want to see
And applaud and
Congratulate it.

And the rest of me will run
Screaming, straight for the door
To feel the wind in my organs, the chill in my bones
Living life
In the raw.

Would you still recognise me, I wonder
The creature within?
Or would you be horrified
At the lidless eyes
And terrible lipless grin?

Would you put on a pleasant face
Curl your toes and take a deep breath
Put out your hand, reaching for mine
And say
It's so nice to finally meet you
In the flesh?

# Depths

Blue, black, blue,
Black, blue, black
Blue…
Falling slowly through life
The lower you sink the greater the pressure
Pressing on you
Blue, black, blue,
Black, blue, black
Blue…
Muffled excuses, echoes of advice
An angry heart pounding on eardrums
Trying to get through
Blue, black, blue,
Black, blue, black
Blue…
Blurry recollections and watery sights
Murky memories of people I knew
Is that you?
Blue, black, blue,
Black, blue, black
Blue…
Suffocating, no escape to be seen
I don't know how to get back
I don't know what to do
Black, blue, black,
Blue, black, blue
Black…

# The Storm is Coming

The streetlamps dribble their orange gloom onto the damp dank
  road below
A half-hearted dew covers the bin bags huddled together
Rubbish flees from under the hedges, scuttling along the
  gumstudded pavement
The crooked crescent cowers behind a curtain of clouds.
The storm is coming.
Rain so heavy it will wash away all the colour from the world
Dragging it down the drains, the darkness drinking it in.
Even the rainbow will be black and white
If the storm ever decides to subside.
If it ever begins.

# The Forest of Fears

Tread carefully in the forest of fears
Lids pressed down tight, eyelashes stitching them closed
The crackling of leaves underfoot
Like the breaking of bones and crushing of dreams
Almost easy
The damp ubiquitous scent of failure
Stings your nostrils and sends a chill running
Like a pointed finger down your spine
Birds cry mocking melodies, painful whispered jeers.
Draw the well-woven covers of comfort and denial
Tight round your shoulders, tighter still.
It's snowing behind your eyelids
Laying another blanket to protect you
To muffle the sound of hope trodden underfoot.
Tread carefully in the forest of fears
For those eyes, if startled, may be ripped open
To find summer in full bloom.

# Diutius

Tempestuous thoughts
Black clouds of a stormy mind
Lightning streaks across a furrowed brow
Echoing thunder
Reverberating through a shivering soul.
A wild wind howls as it tosses the settled leaves
And rain beats down
Behind glassy panes
As the clouds collect overhead.
It rages on.
How long
Until the sun slices through
Or the moon clefts the darkness asunder?
How long?

# A Poet's Legacy

Sometimes I feel I can
Reach through your words
And touch your beating heart
Lay a finger on the pulse of your pen
On your inky blue veins
And see through the windows of your lines
Into your aching, torn, weeping, hurting soul
And then I remember
Your eyes are tightly closed
Under a mound of mud
Your beating heart has turned to dust
And the soil has drunk your blood
And I wonder
Perhaps all you really left was a mirror
And the sorrow is all mine.

# Awaiting Sunrise

I laid my head in the soft lap of night
And I cried all my sorrows to sleep
I pressed my nose and my lips
To the window's cold pane
And my cheek to the autumn of a week
I counted dead stars and the rustles of the breeze
And I answered the cry of every beast
And I whispered back at the moon that wasn't there
Saying I wish I, too, could hide my face
For mirrors stare too hard at me
And my photographs have all withered on the tree of my past
And it's too dark in here, too dark
For new images to develop.

# Who is greater?

My spinning has become nothing but confusion
Blurred vision, wrapped in the dirty white shrouds of the world
Tighter, tighter, faster, faster, lower
The beat is quiet, dead chatter fills my veins
Past, present and future disunited, cleft apart by emptiness.
Deep down, in the murky depths of a stale soul,
I long for that terrifying question
The sweet sting of honesty on my cheek
To slice through the sheets, the shrouds, the shadows
And bring me to my knees
At your feet.

# Morning will come…

I'd like to go out into the night
And throw all my thoughts up at the stars
And try and make sense of their constellations
And see your face smiling back at me in the moon
Illuminating, telling me you understand
I wish to sleep in a cradle of moonlight
And rest my head upon the midnight breeze
And wake to find the world a brighter place
And see that all my darkness has disappeared
As you warm me with your sundrenched smile
And your rays kiss my tousled head, now lighter, free.

# Ache

There's an ache
Like an old wound
Which distraction and distance has healed over
Against my wishes
And when the cold weather comes
It hurts again
So much that I feel like tearing it open
And diving in
To relive those memories
That run in my blood.

# A Need

A burning ache
Bottled acidity
Smothered convulsions
Surging, stifled waves.
A shudder, a shake, a sting
A quiet room
A closed door
A curtain drawn
A deep, soaking breath
A crack
A filling, an emptying
A sob, a sigh
I cry.

# Back to Living

Soon I shall cut loose the noose
Wear it as a necklace, tip the hangman as I leave
I'm going to stroll through the fields, feet bare
Catch mouthfuls of rain to help swallow my pride
Dump my rucksack in a river whose current is the past
And salute the crows for singing to a different tune
I will read into the bold colours of the parting clouds
The italicised shadows
And the underlined eyes of old friends and strangers
Biting my lips, the colours of old bruises
Using the palms of my hands again, now the colour of cold tea
Take out my essence from its carefully worded box
And whirl in it, while it billows in the wind

# Standing

Standing, limb to limb
Hands on chest, one over the other
Desperately trying to resuscitate a deadened heart
So heavy with sin that imprints of each and every toe
   are left on the mat.
Desperately seeking deep breaths
As floor meets head to deliver the kiss of life
Again and again
And again.
Slabs of meat move in mouths
Forming familiar sounds
That I once knew
Before souls became 'I', 'me'.
Stones sing praises louder than I can
Their arches curve in prostration overhead
As the electrifying waves of 'Ameen' wash over me
Let it be, O Lord,
That I see
Let it be, O Lord
That drops of your Mercy and Forgiveness
Fall on me
That this dirtied heart and soul,
Of their bonds of clay, finally
Be free.

# Tears

Streams of hot liquid pressure
From glassy pools
That speak volumes with no lips

The flow
That springs from the heart
Wells up in the eyes
And ends in a river
Cascading down the face
Of the sighing mountain
Of worry, confusion, regret

The reverberations
Palpitations, shakes, uncontrollable sobs
That emanate from an unsettled core

The sharp sting
From pricks to the conscience
The heat behind the shuttered marbles
Downturned...

Dried , at last
By the soft fabric of comfort
Brushed away with a forgiving embrace
Eyes, once again,
Uplifted
By a sincerely smiling face.

# The Colour of Words

The soft yellow whispers that light up the mind and soul,

The vibrant green wisdom that you nurture in the freshly ploughed soil of the heart,

The deep scarlet longing painted across a sunsetting sky the evening before you leave,

The gentle pink promise that you wash away the night with, come morning,

The clear blue droplets of clarity scattered across the grass, which trickle down the windows leaving and yet not leaving a mark,

The flush of purple passion as that sparkling crystal purity is mixed with a throbbing red love, wrapping me in the velvet cloak of your memories,

The deep swallowing darkness which your absence spills across the canvas of my life, leaving everything a shadow of itself.

You are the colour of words, the artist of my soul. Please, come paint my world again.

# A Sip of Remembrance

Coffee tastes like wisdom
And its aroma reminds me of your energy
And late nights which dawn overlapped.
It's sharp, velvet smooth tang
Waltzes with every taste bud on my tongue.
It seeps into my bloodstream
Where it meets with your memories
And knocks on the door of dormant dreams...
It is the sunrise to my sleep
The match to my dry wood
It is the 'yes' to my 'maybes'
And the 'cans' to my 'shoulds'
It is the fuel of lovers and definers of good
Who, the power of this elixir, fully understood.
I drink it because you love it
Though I never thought I could
And now it's my companion,
It sits where you stood
Keeping me awake
Giving my veins a gentle shake
Soothing that chronic ache...
The steam embroiders the air with its savoury scent
With an elegance and grace,
And its strength reminds me
Of your presence
And its warmth of your embrace.

# Stray

Wandering, bedraggled in the alleyways of life
Lost and alone in a world of shadows
You took me in
Though my shoes may have left marks on your floor
And I may have almost emptied your cupboards
A fire and smile I sat before
And I was warmed for the first time
A rinse and a scrub, a brush and clean socks
You walked with me
Hand in hand
To your front door
Out onto the straight road your house lies on
And on the days
When I've strayed
Back down the dark and dingy alleyways
I remember that moment, that smile, that fire
And I somehow I find myself at your front door again
And it's still open.

# About the Author

**A**nna-Maria Fatimah Ramzy is a poet and linguist. She was born in Oxford in the UK, where she grew up. She is currently studying for a Masters in Applied Linguistics at Oxford University, which she hopes to use in the development of Arabic curricula for English speakers.

Her undergraduate degree in Oriental Studies at Oxford, during which she studied both Arabic and Persian, allowed her to delve into the depths of classical and modern Arabic and Persian literature. Though this fuelled her love of poetry, which she had demonstrated from a young age, it was not until she lived in Damascus for a year in 2010 that she uncovered her passion for writing.

It was in Damascus that Anna-Maria met Anse Tamara Gray, her guide, teacher and mentor, and was shown a path of spiritual upbringing that she felt not only united the many strands of her identity, but wove them into a firm handhold. The student-teacher bond that unfolded has been a source of profound guidance, stability and inspiration to her as she has travelled along this path. This is her first collection of poems.

# DAYBREAK PRESS

DAYBREAK PRESS is the publishing arm of Rabata, an international organization dedicated to promoting positive cultural change through the spiritual mentoring of women by women and the revival of the female voice in scholarship. Daybreak is committed to publishing female scholars, activists, and authors in the genres of poetry, fiction and non-fiction. It sponsors the annual New Day writing contest for unpublished female authors and operates the Daybreak Bookstore in St. Paul, Minnesota. For more information please visit Rabata.org/Daybreak.

DAYBREAK PRESS

# Contest

The **New Day Rabata Writers Contest** offers you an opportunity to be heard. Your voice is important, your story matters, and your knowledge can make a difference. Send us your manuscript today!

Daybreak Press seeks to publish the works of previously unpublished female authors with the launch of its New Day annual writing contest.

Topics rotate yearly from poetry to fiction to nonfiction. For 2015, we will be accepting fiction submissions. The deadline for submissions is December 31 each year, and winners will be announced each March.

Grand prize – A publishing package from Daybreak Press that includes author support, professional editing services, typesetting, ISBN assignment, cover design, etc., and a cash prize of $500.00.

For more information please visit http://www.rabata.org/daybreak. We look forward to reading your stories!

## Colophon

**B**REWING STORMS is set in 10.5/13.5 Hypatia Sans Pro, an Adobe geometric sans serif typeface designed by Thomas Phinney in 2002 for the Adobe Originals collection. Named for the classical mathematician, Hypatia of Alexandria (370-415), who was the first woman to make a substantial contribution to the development of mathematics. The capitals have classic Roman proportions while the lower-case exhibits strong geometric tendencies tempered with humanism to increase warmth and legibility. The angled vestigial serifs on the upper left of stems give a modern counterpoint to a design that might otherwise be reminiscent of the 1920s or 1930s.